TV COOKS

Rick Stein

COOKS

Seafood

BBC

Published by BBC Worldwide Limited,
Woodlands, 80 Wood Lane,
London W12 0TT

The recipes in this book first appeared in the following:
Rick Stein's Taste of the Sea
© Richard Stein 1995
Rick Stein's Fruits of the Sea
© Richard Stein 1997

This edition first published 1998
© Richard Stein 1998
The moral right of the author has been asserted

ISBN 0 563 38453 0

Photographs: Juliet Piddington
© BBC Worldwide Limited 1998

Project Editor: Charlotte Lochhead
Copy Editor: Pam Mallender
Design: Town Group Creative
Stylist and Home Economist:
Sarah Ramsbottom
Author photograph: Laurie Evans

Set in New Caledonia and Helvetica
Printed and bound in France by
Imprimerie Pollina S.A., Luçon, France
Colour separations by
Imprimerie Pollina S.A.
Cover printed by Imprimerie Pollina S.A.

Cover and frontispiece:
Grilled Mussels with Charmoula

CONTENTS

RECIPE NOTES

Wash all fresh produce before preparation and peel as necessary.
Spoon measurements are level. Always use proper measuring spoons:
1 teaspoon = 5ml and 1 tablespoon = 15ml.
Never mix metric or imperial measures in one recipe. Stick to one or the other.
Nutritional notes are for a single portion, serving one person when the dish is made for the number of servings stated in the recipe (unless indicated otherwise). The analysis of deep-fried recipes are provided on the basis of an estimated amount of oil absorbed in cooking.
Anyone with an allergy to nuts should substitute groundnut oil for corn oil and walnut oil for olive oil.
Eggs are medium. If your kitchen is warm, keep the eggs in the fridge, but allow them to come to room temperature before using. While the proven risks of healthy people becoming ill from eating fresh raw eggs are minimal, pregnant women, the sick, the elderly and the very young should avoid eating raw or partially cooked eggs.

HANDY CONVERSION TABLES

Weight		Volume		Linear	
15g	½oz	30ml	1fl oz	5mm	¼in
25g	1oz	50ml	2fl oz	10mm/1cm	½in
40g	1½oz	100ml	3½fl oz	2cm	¾in
55g	2oz	125ml	4fl oz	2.5cm	1in
85g	3oz	150ml	5fl oz (¼ pint)	5cm	2in
115g	4oz	175ml	6fl oz	7.5cm	3in
140g	5oz	200ml	7fl oz (⅓ pint)	10cm	4in
175g	6oz	225ml	8fl oz	13cm	5in
200g	7oz	250ml	9fl oz	15cm	6in
225g	8oz	300ml	10fl oz (½ pint)	18cm	7in
250g	9oz	350ml	12fl oz	20cm	8in
280g	10oz	400ml	14fl oz	23cm	9in
350g	12oz	425ml	15fl oz (¾ pint)	25cm	10in
375g	13oz	450ml	16fl oz	28cm	11in
400g	14oz	500ml	18fl oz	30cm	12in
425g	15oz	600ml	20fl oz (1 pint)		
450g	1lb	700ml	1¼ pints	**Oven Temperatures**	
550g	1¼lb	850ml	1½ pints	225F	110C GAS ¼
750g	1lb 10oz	1 litre	1¾ pints	250F	120C GAS ½
900g	2lb	1.2 litres	2 pints	275F	140C GAS 1
1kg	2¼lb	1.3 litres	2¼ pints	300F	150C GAS 2
1.3kg	3lb	1.4 litres	2½ pints	325F	160C GAS 3
1.8kg	4lb	1.7 litres	3 pints	350F	180C GAS 4
2.25kg	5lb	2 litres	3½ pints	375F	190C GAS 5
		2.5 litres	4½ pints	400F	200C GAS 6
				425F	220C GAS 7
				450F	230C GAS 8
				475F	240C GAS 9

ⓕ **Low fat**

I can't visit a seafood stall at a good fishmonger's or market without wanting to buy clams, oysters, mussels, prawns, squid, scallops or lobsters to take home and cook. Enthusiasm for picking things out of shells unites those who enjoy the simple pleasures of life, anyone who likes seafood is bound to be a friend.

I love to come up with ideas that no one may have thought of before in cooking and the recipe that pleases me most in this book is *Whelk Fritters* on page 34. There are more exotic dishes, like *Mussel, Cockle and Clam Masala* and *Seared Scallop Salad with Parma Ham and Croûtons* but I felt that to take the humble whelk and do something different with it, turn it into a delightful shallow-fried, breaded, first course flavoured with tomato, parsley and garlic is a very satisfying achievement.

All the recipes are about enjoyment. What would you think, for example, of moist piles of crab meat served with a salad of small leaves and the lightest of dressings, and beside it some sliced cucumber steeped in a little fish sauce and some delicious tarragon mayonnaise. Doesn't that sound like fun? (See page 57.)

I hope you're going to go out and buy lots of lovely shellfish to cook all these recipes. Supplies are ever improving but it's still hard to get some of the seafood for these recipes, most notably, good fresh live clams, and scallops, squid and langoustine which haven't been frozen. *Ask* for those clams and fresh shellfish. *Demand* the best and we will all benefit from better seafood on sale everywhere.

Rick Stein

INGREDIENTS

Butter
Most of my cooking is done with unsalted butter. This is because salted butter tends to increase the amount of salt in a recipe and because I prefer the flavour. Nevertheless, sometimes it doesn't really matter which you use, in which case the recipe will just say butter. Salted butter is still significantly cheaper than unsalted because it keeps much better.

Clams
Until recently it was virtually impossible to get any clams in Britain except the large, hard-shelled clam, which is only really useful for chowders. All the delightful little clams that you get in France, the *palourdes*, the *praires* and *vernis*, were unavailable. Now things are beginning to improve.

Crabs
If the meat of a crab came out of the shell in the same solid chunks as lobster it would, without doubt, fetch the same sort of price. It is as sweet and full of flavour as lobster, but it comes out in small flakes. Crab is delicate and a common error is to partner it with overpowering flavours so the taste is lost completely. When writing my own recipes, I have kept that thought in mind.

Fresh root ginger
This looks rather like a gnarled Jerusalem artichoke and ranges from 7.5–15cm/3–6in in length. It has a golden-beige, thin, papery dry skin and is peeled before use. Look for 'roots' that are firm, solid and unmarked, with no signs of shrivelling.

Langoustine
A couple of tips about the quality of langoustine on sale these days. They are much more akin to lobsters than prawns and look like lobsters. Also, like lobsters, their flesh deteriorates very quickly after death. It becomes soft like cotton wool. It is easy to tell if they are fresh – pull back their tails, if they have a good degree of spring in them the meat inside will be firm. If the tail stays spread out when you pull it, the meat will be soft. Be governed by your sense of smell, they should smell sweet and appetising. If there is any suggestion of sourness or worse still, ammonia, don't buy them.

Lemon grass
I think this is the single most recognizable flavour in Thai cooking, the thick, moist stem of a tropical grass with a lovely lemony taste and smell. It also makes a delicious savoury butter to serve with grilled lemon sole fillets. Incidentally, lemon grass does grow reasonably well in greenhouses over here and even outdoors in summer. Just buy a stem or two and put in moist potting compost. There is no real alternative to lemon grass but, at a push, you could use pared lemon rind.

Lobsters
British lobsters are the best in the world. I have tried spiny lobsters in the Mediterranean, Southeast Asia and Australia, and I have tried lobsters from the Eastern seaboard of the United States and Canada and I now know, without doubt, that ours are the sweetest and richest of all seafood. I regard lobster as the same calibre of delicacy as caviar or truffles. For the amount of work that goes into catching them, I think they are astonishingly good value for money. Canadian or American lobsters, which are now available live and air-freighted into the UK are, however, a good buy for dishes where the meat is taken out of the shell and served with other ingredients.

Mussels

Most mussels available in fishmongers and supermarkets with fish counters are rope-grown. That means the spats (the mussel seeds) are encouraged to attach their threads to ropes suspended in the sea. You can tell whether those you buy are rope-grown or not by the occasional strands of rope still attached to the mussel. A great advantage of rope-grown mussels is that they tend to be relatively clean and free of barnacles and weed. Those harvested from rocks tend to be harder to clean. As to flavour, the rope-grown ones tend to be sweet and plump, the rock ones more seaweedy and ozoney. There is no need to steep them in water after buying. The shells only open when they sense they are in well aerated, brackish or sea water.

Oysters

There are two types of oyster on sale in Britain, the Native (or European) and Pacific, with the Native oyster usually costing twice as much as the Pacific. It fetches such a high price because it takes much longer to grow; the faster growing Pacific is favoured by the commercial growers.

Prawns

Good quality, large, cooked and raw prawns are now easily available.
North Atlantic prawns: these are the most commonly seen in fishmongers and are sold peeled or in the shell.
Mediterranean prawns (crevettes): these are long, thin prawns with very curly antennae, usually sold cooked. The larger ones usually come from the waters of Madagascar.
Tiger and other raw prawns: I have rather unceremoniously lumped together all the raw prawns which make up a number of species. In Australia they have 13 different commercial species, all of which are probably represented somewhere in what you buy in fishmongers and supermarkets, both frozen and chilled.

Scallops

Scallops are one of our most delicious shellfish – sweet and firm and relatively cheap. Only buy fresh scallops and steer clear of frozen ones, since they have often been soaked in water before freezing to increase their size and make the price seem more attractive. When they thaw out, the water drains out of them, along with a great deal of their flavour.

Sesame oil

I use both cold-pressed and roasted sesame oil. Cold-pressed is light, delicate and fragrant, whereas roasted sesame oil, which is much stronger, is ideal for robust dishes full of spice.

Sichuan pepper

This is a characteristic flavour of Chinese cookery, which manages to be both peppery hot and yet slightly tart and has the effect of numbing the mouth a little. Also called anise pepper, it is not in fact a true pepper but comes from a type of ash tree.

Squid

Squid is much underrated. It has a delicious flavour, more akin to lobster or crab than fish, and deserves to be much more popular. Like cuttlefish and octopus, it belongs to the group known as cephalopods which means 'head-footed', referring to the way the tentacles come out of the head.

1. Thai fish sauce
2. Tamarind pulp
3. Sichuan peppercorns
4. Saffron
5. Oysters
6. Scallops
7. Whelks
8. Clams
9. Cockles
10. Raw Tiger prawns
11. Cooked Mediterranean prawns
12. Cooked North Atlantic prawns
13. Squid
14. Squid rings
15. Cooked lobster
16. Langoustine
17. Whole cooked crab
18. Lemon grass
19. Brown crab meat
20. White crab meat
21. Mussels
22. Feta cheese
23. Root ginger
24. Rocket
25. Salted black beans
26. Rice-shaped pasta

Soups & Stews

CLAM CHOWDER WITH COD

A simple, and perfect, creamy soup. Any clams will do and if you can't get fresh clams in their shells, frozen clam meats are acceptable. When we can get them, we use razorshell clams, so called because they look like old cut-throat razors. They have a beautiful sweet flavour.

Serves 4

16 large or 32 small fresh clams, washed and scrubbed, or frozen clam meats, thawed and cut into 1cm/½in slices

25g/1oz butter

55g/2oz salt pork or thickly sliced green bacon, cut into small dice (See Tip)

115g/4oz onions, diced

225g/8oz potatoes, diced but not washed (See Tip)

300ml/½ pint milk

125ml/4fl oz double cream

1 fresh bay leaf, cut into fine shreds, or 1 dried bay leaf, crushed

115g/4oz skinless cod fillet, cut into 1cm/½in pieces

salt and freshly ground white pepper

1 tbsp chopped fresh parsley and 2 water biscuits, broken into little pieces, to garnish

1 If using fresh clams, place in a large pan with a splash of water. Cover tightly and cook over a high heat. As soon as the clams open, remove the pan from the heat and strain into a colander, set over a bowl. Reserve the cooking liquor. When cool enough to handle, remove the clams from their shells and cut the meat into 1cm/½in slices.

2 Melt the butter in a pan, then fry the diced pork or bacon until it starts to brown. Add the onions and fry until softened.

3 Place the potatoes in a large pan with the milk, cream and bay leaf. Bring to the boil, then reduce to a slow simmer until just cooked but still firm.

4 Add the pork, onions and clam cooking liquor to the potatoes and simmer for 5 minutes, then add the cod fillet. Simmer until the cod is cooked, then add the fresh cooked or thawed clams. Thoroughly warm through, and season with salt, if necessary, and white pepper. Pour into a serving tureen, then garnish with the chopped parsley and broken water biscuits.

Nutrition notes per serving: *442 Calories, Protein 20g, Carbohydrate 24g, Fat 30g, Saturated fat 17g, Fibre 1g, Added sugar 0g, Salt 2.66g.*

TIP

You can make salt pork by simply sprinkling 15g/½oz salt over a 55g/2oz slice of pork loin 30 minutes before using. Because you need the starch to thicken the liquid, don't wash the potatoes after they are cut.

A SMALL STEW OF BASS, SQUID, MUSSELS AND PRAWNS WITH A WARM AIOLI SAUCE

Serves 4

4 large cooked Mediterranean prawns (*crevettes*) in their shells

12 mussels, cleaned
(See Tip, page 17)

1 orange

1 tsp fresh lemon juice

2 plum tomatoes, roughly chopped

6 tbsp Olive oil mayonnaise (See Tip)

3 garlic cloves, crushed with a little salt

2 tbsp double cream

175g/6oz sea bass fillet, skin on, cut into 8 thin slices

115g/4oz prepared squid, cut into rings (See Tip, page 42)

1 tsp finely chopped fresh flatleaf parsley

salt and freshly ground black pepper

FOR THE ROASTED FISH STOCK

25g/1oz butter

1kg/2¼lb fish bones, such as lemon sole, brill and plaice

115g/4oz each of onions, celery and carrots, chopped

1 tsp chopped fresh thyme

1 Remove the shells from the prawns and reserve. Cut the prawns in half lengthways. Make the fish stock: preheat the oven to 200C/400F/Gas 6. Melt the butter in a large roasting tin. Add the fish bones, prawn shells, vegetables and thyme, and turn them over a few times until they are well coated in the butter. Roast for 30 minutes, then transfer to a pan.

2 Add 2.25 litres/4 pints water to the pan and bring to the boil. Simmer for 20 minutes, then strain through a sieve lined with muslin into a clean pan. Bring back to the boil and boil until reduced to about 1.2 litres/2 pints.

3 Place the mussels in a large pan with a splash of the stock, then cover and cook over a high heat for 3–4 minutes until they have opened. Discard any that remain closed. Strain most of the mussel cooking liquor through a sieve, into the stock, discarding any grit. Cover the mussels and keep warm.

4 Remove a strip of rind from the orange with a potato peeler, then squeeze out the juice from the orange. Place 850ml/1½ pints of fish stock, the orange rind, two tablespoons of orange juice, the lemon juice and the tomatoes in a large pan. Bring to the boil and simmer for 15 minutes, until reduced to 600ml/ 1 pint. Strain into a jug and discard the solids.

5 Preheat the grill to high. Place the mayonnaise, garlic and cream into a bowl, add a good splash of warm stock and stir together until smooth. Gradually stir in the remaining stock. Return the mixture to the pan and heat gently to the temperature of egg custard (hot enough to be just uncomfortable to your little finger), stirring all the time until slightly thickened. Remove from the heat, stir in half a teaspoon of salt and keep warm.

6 Place the sea bass and squid on to the greased rack of a grill pan and sprinkle with a little salt and pepper. Grill for 2 minutes, adding the prawns towards the end to warm through. Arrange the seafood in four warmed soup bowls and surround with the warm garlic cream sauce, then sprinkle with parsley.

Nutrition notes per serving: *588 Calories, Protein 28g, Carbohydrate 7g, Fat 50g, Saturated fat 8g, Fibre 1g, Added sugar 0g, Salt 3.13g.*

TIP

To make Olive oil mayonnaise ensure all the ingredients are at room temperature. Place two egg yolks, two teaspoons of white wine vinegar and half a teaspoon of salt in a bowl. Using a wire whisk, beat 300ml/½ pint of olive oil into the yolks a few drops at a time. Once you have added about the same volume of oil as the original egg mixture, you can add the oil more quickly.

CAUTION! This recipe contains raw eggs.

MUSSELS WITH TURMERIC, CUMIN AND CORIANDER Ⓕ

Serves 4

¼ tsp coriander seeds

¼ tsp cumin seeds

1kg/2¼lb mussels, cleaned
(See Tip, page 17)

50ml/2fl oz dry white wine

55g/2oz unsalted butter

2 shallots, finely chopped

¼ tsp turmeric

¼ tsp cayenne pepper

600ml/1 pint Fish stock (page 62)

125ml/4fl oz double cream

2 tsp plain flour mixed with
2 tsp softened butter

salt and freshly ground black pepper

1   Dry-fry the coriander and cumin seeds in a dry frying pan over a high heat until they release their aromas. Tip into a pestle and mortar or a coffee grinder and grind to a fine powder.

2   Place the mussels in a large pan with the wine, cover and cook over a high heat for 3–4 minutes, shaking the pan occasionally, until they have opened. Discard any that remain closed. Strain into a colander, set over a bowl. Reserve the cooking liquor. When cool enough to handle, shell two-thirds and set all the mussels aside.

3   Heat half the butter in a large pan. Add the shallots and fry for 2 minutes or until softened but not browned. Add the ground roasted spices with the turmeric and cayenne pepper and fry for 1 minute.

4   Add the stock and most of the mussel cooking liquor (discard the remainder as it may be gritty) to the pan with the cream and the remaining butter, then whisk in the flour-and-butter paste. Simmer for 10 minutes. Add the mussels and warm through. Season if necessary.

Nutrition notes per serving: *320 Calories, Protein 11g, Carbohydrate 4g, Fat 28g, Saturated fat 17g, Fibre trace, Added sugar 0g, Salt 1.33g.*

BASQUE SQUID STEW Ⓕ

Serves 4

750g/1lb 10oz cleaned squid
(See Tip, page 42)

3 tbsp olive oil

1 onion, chopped

3 garlic cloves, finely chopped

400g can chopped tomatoes

150ml/¼ pint red wine

1 tsp chopped fresh thyme

1 tsp salt

20 turns of the black pepper mill

parsley, to garnish

1   Cut the squid pouches across into rings and separate the tentacles if large. Heat the oil in a large, heavy-based pan, add the squid and cook over a high heat, stirring occasionally, until lightly browned.

2   Add the onion and garlic to the pan and cook for 5 minutes or until softened. Stir in the tomatoes, wine, 300ml/½ pint of water and the thyme and bring up to the boil. Cover and simmer very gently for 2 hours. Season with the salt and pepper and sprinkle with parsley before serving.

Nutrition notes per serving: *268 Calories, Protein 31g, Carbohydrate 8g, Fat 10g, Saturated fat 1g, Fibre 1g, Added sugar 0g, Salt 2.18g.*

TIP

I would call this the *boeuf bourguignon* of fish stews – it is so deep and rich and the squid becomes very tender after long, slow cooking. This dish is great eaten on its own with French bread or used as a base for a more substantial fish stew. Add extra seafood such as seasoned sliced scallops, halved, small, skinless flat-fish fillets, langoustines, large prawns or pieces of cooked lobster. Bring back to the boil and simmer for 2 minutes to warm through.

Starters

MUSSELS WITH TOMATO, CELERY AND SAFFRON BUTTER

This recipe uses mussel shells as natural containers for serving at a party, without need of knives, forks or plates. The mussels are served on the half shell with a rich saffron butter sauce, some finely chopped celery that has been lightly cooked so it is still a little crunchy, and some finely diced, good sweet tomatoes.

Serves 4

900g/2lb mussels, cleaned (See Tip)

50ml/2fl oz dry white wine

600ml/1 pint Fish stock (page 62)

¼ tsp saffron strands

85g/3oz inner celery sticks, finely diced

3 tomatoes, skinned, seeded and finely diced

175g/6oz chilled unsalted butter, cut into small pieces

juice of ¼ lemon

salt and freshly ground black pepper

1   Place the mussels in a large pan with one tablespoon of the wine. Cover and cook over a high heat for 3–4 minutes, shaking the pan occasionally, until the mussels have opened. Discard any that remain closed. Strain into a colander, set over a bowl, holding back the last tablespoon or so of liquor, which may be gritty. Stir two tablespoons of the cooking liquor into the fish stock and discard the remainder.

2   Bring the stock, the remaining wine and the saffron to the boil and boil rapidly until reduced to about four tablespoons. Bring a small pan of salted water to the boil, add the celery and cook for 1 minute. Drain and refresh under cold running water, then set aside.

3   Preheat the oven to 140C/275F/Gas 1. Remove the top half of each mussel shell, leaving the mussel in the other half. Lay side by side in a shallow ovenproof serving dish. Spoon the celery and tomatoes on top of the mussels and season with a little salt and pepper. (This can be done up to 1 hour in advance, but don't place cooked mussels in the fridge, as they never taste the same again. Simply cover with plastic film to stop them from drying out.)

4   When you are ready to serve, remove the plastic film and cover the mussels with foil, then warm through in the oven for a few minutes. Meanwhile, bring the reduced fish stock back to the boil and over a high heat whisk in the cold butter pieces, a few at a time. If the sauce separates, add a little more water, bring it back to the boil and it will cohere again. Stir in the lemon juice and season to taste. Remove the mussels from the oven, uncover, and spoon over a little sauce, then serve immediately.

Nutrition notes per serving: *393 Calories, Protein 10g, Carbohydrate 2g, Fat 37g, Saturated fat 23g, Fibre 1g, Added sugar 0g, Salt 1.29g.*

TIP

To clean mussels: wash in plenty of cold water and scrub the shells with a stiff brush. Use a knife to scrape off any barnacles that are sticking to them. Discard any open mussels that do not close when lightly tapped on the work surface. Pull out the tough, fibrous beards protruding from the tightly closed shells.

THE FINEST SEAFOOD IN A SMALL RAGOUT
WITH A DEEP RED WINE SAUCE

This is unashamedly a real show-off dish. The quantities are small but the seafood is the best and the sauce contains an expensive amount of red wine, reduced by boiling to give the richest, deepest flavour imaginable. Some people are put off by the idea of fish in a red wine sauce but when wine and fish are joined as the dish is served and the red wine has been reduced and sweetened with port, then finished with butter, the combination is irresistible.

Serves 4

1 cooked lobster, weighing about 450g/1lb

4 small skinless Dover sole fillets

**4 prepared scallops
(See Tip, page 38)**

salt and freshly ground black pepper

pinch of paprika

FOR THE CROÛTONS

2 medium thick slices white bread

2 tbsp sunflower oil

small knob unsalted butter

FOR THE RED WINE SAUCE

600ml/1 pint Fish stock (page 62)

600ml/1 pint red wine

125ml/4fl oz port

85g/3oz chilled unsalted butter, cut into small pieces

1 Remove the meat from the lobster (See Tip), trying to remove the claw meat in as large pieces as possible. Slice the tail meat across in 1cm/½in-thick pieces. Lay the Dover sole fillets and scallops on the lightly greased rack of a grill pan and season with a little salt and pepper and the paprika. This will give them a pleasing colour.

2 Make the croûtons: using a 5cm/2in plain pastry cutter, cut out four rounds from the bread slices. Heat the oil and butter in a frying pan and fry the rounds for 1–2 minutes on each side, until golden. Drain on kitchen paper and keep warm.

3 Make the sauce: place the stock, wine and port in a pan and bring to the boil. Boil rapidly until reduced to about 125ml/4fl oz. Whisk in the butter a little at a time and keep warm over a low heat.

4 Preheat the grill to high, then grill the Dover sole and scallops for 2 minutes. Add the lobster meat pieces and grill for 1 minute to warm through. Pile the seafood into the centre of four warmed plates, drizzle over some of the sauce and pour more round the edges. Lay a croûton on top of each pile.

Nutrition notes per serving: *570 Calories, Protein 36g, Carbohydrate 12g, Fat 27g, Saturated fat 13g, Fibre trace, Added sugar 4g, Salt 1.82g.*

TIP

You can, of course, ask your fishmonger to remove the meat from a cooked lobster if you give him enough notice of what you need. If you want to try it yourself, twist off the larger claw arms and the legs. Cut away any bands binding the claws together. Break the claw arms apart at the joints, then crack the shell with the back of a knife blade or a hammer. Remove the meat from each section of the claws in as large pieces as possible. As you need the tail meat in one piece for slicing, detach the head from the tail, then cut the head in half and remove the tomalley (liver) and any roe (these are edible). Turn the tail section over and cut along either side of the flat under-shell with scissors. Lift back the flap and remove the meat. Slice as needed and remove the intestinal tract from each slice with the point of a sharp knife.

CHAR-GRILLED TIGER PRAWNS WITH LEMON GRASS, CHILLI AND CORIANDER Ⓕ

Tiger prawns are now being farmed in large quantities in Thailand. They are easy to buy here and you should be able to get all the ingredients to make this first course, including some bamboo skewers for a really authentic touch at most large supermarkets or an oriental food shop. This dish is best cooked on a barbecue, but can also be cooked successfully under the grill, if you prefer.

Serves 4

20 raw tiger prawns or king prawns, in their shells and headless, each weighing about 25g/1oz

30ml/1fl oz groundnut oil, seasoned with 1 tsp salt and freshly ground black pepper

FOR THE DRESSING

30ml/1fl oz Thai fish sauce (*nam pla*; See Tip)

1 mild Dutch green chilli, seeded and finely chopped

1 fresh lemon grass stick

juice of 1 lemon

½ tsp sugar

FOR THE SALAD

small bunch fresh coriander

½ iceberg lettuce, finely sliced

1 Light the barbecue at least 30 minutes before you want to start cooking. The secret of successful barbecuing lies in getting the grill bar so hot that anything you put on it sears and carbonizes quickly and so doesn't stick. If you are using bamboo skewers, soak them in cold water for 30 minutes to stop them from catching light on the barbecue or under the grill.

2 Remove the shells from the prawns, except for the last small piece on the end of the tail. Cut the bodies in half lengthways, leaving them joined at the tail. Using a pastry brush, paint the prawns liberally with the seasoned oil. Thread five prawns on to each skewer and set aside until needed.

3 Make the dressing: in a bowl mix together the fish sauce, 150ml/¼ pint of water and the chilli. Remove the coarse outer leaves from the lemon grass and finely slice the more tender centre; don't be too purist as all lemon grass is fairly stringy. Add to the dressing with the lemon juice and sugar.

4 Pick off about 20 of the best coriander leaves to use in the salad and reserve. Chop the remainder finely and set aside.

5 Barbecue or grill the prawns for exactly 5 minutes, turning them half-way through the cooking time. Warm the dressing over a gentle heat and add the chopped coriander to the pan just before taking it off the heat. Place the whole coriander leaves and lettuce on serving plates, top with the skewered prawns and spoon over the dressing.

Nutrition notes per serving: *160 Calories, Protein 18g, Carbohydrate 4g, Fat 8g, Saturated fat 1g, Fibre trace, Added sugar 1g, Salt 1.27g.*

TIP

Fish sauce, or *nam pla*, as it is known in Thailand, is a salty fish liquid derived from the salting of anchovies. It is an essential ingredient in Thai and other Southeast Asian cuisines. It has a slightly fishy but not unpleasant salty taste and is available in most supermarkets. It should be fairly clear and not too brown. If you can't find any, the best alternatives are a light soy sauce or anchovy essence.

CAUTION! This recipe contains nuts (oil).

MUSSELS WITH A CREAM AND WHITE WINE SABAYON

Serves 4

½ onion, sliced

1 small bay leaf

150ml/¼ pint dry white wine

1.8kg/4lb mussels, cleaned
(See Tip, page 17)

3 medium egg yolks

150ml/¼ pint double cream

115g/4oz cold unsalted butter,
cut into small pieces

squeeze of fresh lemon juice

salt and freshly ground white pepper

2 tbsp chopped fresh parsley,
to serve

1   Place the onion, bay leaf and wine into a large pan. Bring up to the boil and simmer for 5 minutes. Add the mussels, cover and cook over a high heat for 3–4 minutes until the mussels have opened. Discard any that remain closed. Using a slotted spoon, lift the mussels into a large serving dish, cover and keep warm. Reserve the cooking liquor.

2   Bring a pan of water to a gentle simmer. In a large heatproof bowl (which will sit on top of the pan) whisk together the egg yolks and cream. Strain most of the mussel cooking liquor (to catch any grit) through a sieve lined with muslin into the bowl and set the bowl over the simmering water. Whisk briskly until the mixture is light and frothy. Do not let the sauce get too hot or it will curdle.

3   Whisk in the butter, a little at a time. Remove the bowl from the heat and season to taste with lemon juice, salt and pepper. Pour the sauce over the mussels and sprinkle with the parsley.

Nutrition notes per serving: *549 Calories, Protein 20g, Carbohydrate 3g, Fat 48g, Saturated fat 28g, Fibre trace, Added sugar 0g, Salt 1.31g.*

CAUTION! This recipe contains lightly cooked eggs.

PRAWNS FRIED WITH GARLIC BUTTER

Serves 4

2 large garlic cloves, roughly
chopped

115g/4oz unsalted butter, softened

1 tsp fresh lemon juice

1 tsp brandy

24 large cooked prawns, in their
shells

salt and freshly ground black pepper

15g/½oz chopped fresh parsley

1   Make the garlic butter: add a good pinch of salt to the garlic and crush to a paste with the back of a knife. Mix with the butter, lemon juice and brandy.

2   Melt 25g/1oz of the garlic butter in a large frying pan. Add the prawns and gently fry for 2 minutes or until heated through. Season with salt and pepper.

3   Stir the parsley into the remaining garlic butter, add to the pan and, when it is hot and foaming, spoon the prawns and butter into four warm shallow dishes.

Nutrition notes per serving: *271 Calories, Protein 11g, Carbohydrate 1g, Fat 24g, Saturated fat 15g, Fibre trace, Added sugar 0g, Salt 2.19g.*

TIP

Flavoured butters are perfect sliced into rounds and placed on grilled fish. They are also ideal for flavouring sauces and stuffing fish fillets. Simply blend together flavouring ingredients and softened butter, then turn out on to a sheet of plastic film or greaseproof paper, roll into a sausage shape and chill. Try mustard butter with trout, a roasted red pepper, sun-dried tomato and red chilli butter with red mullet, or anchovy butter with cod fillets. Pop the fish topped with butter under a hot grill for 30 seconds before serving.

CHINESE WHELKS WITH BEANSPROUTS
AND BUTTON MUSHROOMS ⓕ

Serves 4

3 tbsp sunflower oil

3 garlic cloves, very finely chopped

5cm/2in piece fresh root ginger, very finely chopped

1 large red finger chilli, seeded and sliced

225g/8oz shelled whelks, thinly sliced

115g/4oz button mushrooms, thinly sliced

55g/2oz mustard greens or pak choi, coarsely shredded

55g/2oz beansprouts

2 tbsp oyster sauce

½ tbsp light soy sauce

2 tbsp dry sherry or rice wine (See Tip, page 37)

1   Heat the oil in a wok or large deep frying pan. Add the garlic, ginger and chilli and stir fry over a high heat for 30 seconds until softened. Add the whelks and stir fry for 1 minute.

2   Add the mushrooms and stir fry for 30 seconds, then add the mustard greens or pak choi and the beansprouts and stir fry for 30 seconds until the leaves have just wilted into the bottom of the pan. Stir in the oyster sauce, soy sauce and sherry or rice wine and cook for 1 minute.

Nutrition notes per serving: *157 Calories, Protein 12g, Carbohydrate 3g, Fat 10g, Saturated fat 1g, Fibre 1g, Added sugar trace, Salt 1.46g.*

TIP

Traditionally, whelks are served with malt vinegar, freshly ground white pepper and lots of fresh brown bread and butter. But actually, they're incredibly good thinly sliced and stirred into a Chinese stir fry. This dish also makes a lovely light lunch or supper served with steamed rice or noodles.

SCALLOPS WITH BASIL, SAFFRON AND PASTA

Serves 4

600ml/1 pint Fish stock (page 62)

50ml/2fl oz white wine

good pinch of saffron

150ml/¼ pint double cream

55g/2oz unsalted butter

115g/4oz thin fresh or dried pasta such as vermicelli or fedilini

knob of butter

6 fresh basil leaves, finely sliced

12 scallop shells, to serve

12 good-sized scallops, halved

1   Make the sauce: place the stock, wine and saffron in a pan and boil rapidly to reduce by three-quarters. Add the cream, whisk in the butter and reduce further until the sauce coats the back of the spoon.

2   Cook the pasta in lightly salted water according to packet instructions until tender but firm to the bite (*al dente*). Drain and toss in the knob of butter with the fresh basil leaves. Keep warm.

3   Preheat the grill to medium and warm the scallop shells for a few moments, then arrange on plates and divide the pasta between the shells. Bring the sauce to the boil, add the scallops, reduce the heat and poach for 2 minutes, then spoon into the shells.

Nutrition notes per serving: *630 Calories, Protein 36g, Carbohydrate 23g, Fat 45g, Saturated fat 27g, Fibre 1g, Added sugar 0g, Salt 1.68g.*

Quick & Simple

BASQUE-STYLE STUFFED CRAB

I like using shells as natural containers for seafood. Mussels, scallops, clams and crabs all look much more appetising to me presented in this way. The great charm of *shangurro*, which comes from the Basque coast of Northern Spain, is that in San Sebastian, Santander and Bilbao it is normally served using the back shell of a spider crab as a gratin dish to hold the combination of spider crab meat, tomato, garlic, chilli, olive oil, parsley and breadcrumbs. I must admit, however, that if you have time to pick out the meat from four spider crabs, you would hardly call this a quick and simple dish. This recipe is so good though, it is still delicious when made using brown crab meat instead of spider crab. It's nice for each person to have their own crab, but if you can't get the right size crabs, use two or three slightly bigger ones and let everyone help themselves at the table.

Serves 4

4 x 450-550g/1-1¼lb cooked brown crabs, or approximately 450g/1lb white crab meat and 115g/4oz brown crab meat (See Tip)

3 tbsp olive oil

2 onions, finely chopped

9 small garlic cloves, finely chopped

225g/8oz plum tomatoes, skinned, seeded and chopped

50ml/2fl oz dry white wine

1 tsp caster sugar

¼ tsp dried chilli flakes

salt and freshly ground black pepper

3 tbsp chopped fresh parsley

55g/2oz fresh white breadcrumbs

15g/½oz butter, melted

1 Preheat the oven to 200C/400F/Gas 6. If using cooked crabs, remove the meat from the shells. Wash out the back shells, then break away the edge along the visible natural line to give a flat open shell. Set aside.

2 Heat the oil in a heavy-based frying pan, then add the onions and eight of the garlic cloves. Fry over a gentle heat for 2 minutes until softened. Increase the heat, add the tomatoes, wine, sugar and chilli flakes, and season with salt and pepper. Simmer for 4 minutes, until the mixture has reduced to a thick sauce.

3 Stir in two tablespoons of the parsley and all the flaked crab meat and spoon the mixture into the crab shells, if using, or individual gratin dishes. If using shells, rest them in a shallow ovenproof dish to stop them from tipping over.

4 Mix the breadcrumbs with the melted butter and the remaining parsley and garlic, then sprinkle over the crab and bake for 10 minutes or until the topping is crisp and golden.

Nutrition notes per serving: *392 Calories, Protein 32g, Carbohydrate 21g, Fat 19g, Saturated fat 4g, Fibre 3g, Added sugar 1g, Salt 1.95g.*

TIP

Although I tend to say that freshly dressed crab meat is best, I think that either chilled pasteurised crab meat or frozen is a perfectly good substitute, since the task of dressing crabs is time-consuming. Personally, though, when time allows, I like jobs like picking crab. I get myself a couple of bowls and a bucket for the debris, pour myself a glass of wine, put on some Mozart, then sit outside next to the herb garden and relax.

MOULES MARINIÈRE

Serves 4

1.6kg/3½lb or 3.9 litres/7 pints mussels, cleaned (See Tip, page17)

55g/2oz unsalted butter

1 onion, chopped

50ml/2fl oz dry white wine

1 tbsp roughly chopped fresh parsley, to serve

1   Place the mussels in a large pan with the butter, onion, white wine and half the parsley and set over a fierce heat for 3–4 minutes. Turn the mussels over every now and then as they start to open. Keep the lid on the pan between turning them.

2   When they are all open remove from the heat and leave for 30 seconds or so to let all the grit settle to the bottom of the pan. Using a large slotted spoon, scoop out the mussels and divide between four large, deep plates. Discard any that remain closed. Pour over the juices from the pan, holding back the last tablespoon or so which may be full of grit, then sprinkle over the parsley.

Nutrition notes per serving: *201 Calories, Protein 15g, Carbohydrate 2g, Fat 14g, Saturated fat 8g, Fibre trace, Added sugar 0g, Salt 0.89g.*

TIP

Moules et Frites (mussels and chips) served with mayonnaise has long been one of my favourite dishes. Serve these mussels with chips, adding a tablespoon of made English mustard to the Olive oil mayonnaise on page 13, or with some fresh baguettes and a bottle of Muscadet.

GRILLED LANGOUSTINE WITH CREAMED GARLIC AND CHIVES

Serves 4

1 large bulb garlic

150ml/¼ pint double cream

1 tbsp Thai fish sauce (*nam pla;* See Tip, page 21)

juice of ½ lemon

24 good-sized raw or cooked langoustine in their shells

30ml/1fl oz oil infused with 1 crushed garlic clove, for grilling

1 tbsp snipped fresh chives

1   Remove the garlic cloves from the bulb, but do not peel them. Place in a pan with 150ml/¼ pint water and cook very gently over a low heat until soft. Squeeze the flesh out of the skins into a liquidiser, add the cooking water and blend until smooth. Add this, the cream, fish sauce and lemon juice to the pan, and warm through over a gentle heat.

2   Preheat the grill to hot. Brush the langoustine with the garlic oil and grill until the shells begin to char. If you are using cooked langoustine, this will be long enough to heat them through. If you are using raw langoustine, they will need a little longer, about 5 minutes in total. When ready to serve, add the chives to the warm garlic sauce, arrange the langoustine on a plate, and spoon over the sauce.

Nutrition notes per serving: *333 Calories, Protein 21g, Carbohydrate 3g, Fat 26g, Saturated fat 12g, Fibre trace, Added sugar 0g, Salt 1.00g.*

GRILLED MUSSELS WITH *CHARMOULA*

Serves 4

60 large mussels, cleaned (See Tip, page 17)

splash of dry white wine or water

25g/1oz finely chopped almonds (optional)

FOR THE *CHARMOULA*

2 tbsp roughly chopped fresh coriander

3 garlic cloves, chopped

1½ tsp ground cumin

½ red chilli, seeded and chopped

½ tsp saffron strands

4 tbsp extra virgin olive oil

juice of 1 lemon

1½ tsp paprika

2 tsp salt

1 Open the mussels by steaming with the wine or water in a covered pan over a fierce heat for 3–4 minutes. Remove from the heat as soon as they have opened. Discard any that remain closed. Reserve the cooking liquor.

2 When the mussels are cool enough to handle, discard one side of the shell. Strain most of the cooking liquor (to catch any grit) through a sieve lined with muslin into a small pan and reduce to about one tablespoon by rapid boiling.

3 Place all the *charmoula* ingredients with the reduced liquor in a liquidiser or food processor and blend until thoroughly mixed. Stir in the chopped almonds, if using.

4 Preheat the grill to high. Arrange the mussels in the grill pan. Spoon a little of the *charmoula* into each mussel shell and grill for about 1 minute until heated through.

Nutrition notes per serving: *236 Calories, Protein 17g, Carbohydrate 2g, Fat 17g, Saturated fat 2g, Fibre 1g, Added sugar 0g, Salt 3.37g.*

TIP

These mussels are also delicious filled with a garlic, basil and pine-nut pesto, which should be made quite dry and coarse (more like a stuffing than a sauce). For the pesto: place 15g/½oz fresh basil, two large garlic cloves, 175ml/6fl oz olive oil, 15g/½oz Parmesan and 15g/½oz pine nuts with the reduced cooking liquor in a food processor or mortar and pestle. Blend until roughly chopped. Fill the shells as before and sprinkle them with breadcrumbs made from two slices of white bread. You can make various other grilled mussel dishes in the same way using flavoured butters such as the garlic butter served with prawns (page 22) or the Coriander and hazelnut butter (page 62).

CAUTION! This recipe contains nuts.

MUSSEL, COCKLE AND CLAM MASALA

I have specified rather more masala paste than you may feel you need for this recipe as the chillies already make it very hot, but if you like your Indian food hot then use it all or use to taste. This dish is best cooked in a wok.

Serves 4

30ml/1fl oz vegetable oil

1.6kg/3½lb or 3.9 litres/7 pints mixed mussels, clams and cockles, cleaned and washed

2 tbsp chopped fresh coriander leaves

FOR THE MASALA

1 tbsp coriander seeds

1 tsp whole cloves

2 tbsp cumin seeds

350g/12oz onions, finely chopped

8 large garlic cloves

55g/2oz fresh root ginger, chopped

walnut-sized knob of dried tamarind pulp (See Tip)

1 tsp turmeric

3 fresh red chillies

2 tbsp red wine vinegar

3 tbsp coconut cream

1 Make the masala: dry-fry the coriander seeds and cloves in a wok or large frying pan over a medium heat for a few minutes, then add the cumin seeds, heating them for 30 seconds. Grind in a clean coffee grinder or mortar and pestle, then place in a food processor with the remaining masala ingredients. Blend to a paste. If the mixture is too stiff, add a little vegetable oil to loosen. Heat the vegetable oil in a wok. Add the masala and fry until the spices separate from the oil.

2 Toss the mussels, clams and cockles into the wok or pan, then cover with a lid and, shaking from time to time, steam-cook until the shells open. Discard any that remain closed. If you feel the mussels haven't produced enough liquid, add a little water. The recipe contains no salt as mussels are salty, but taste to check seasoning. Throw in the coriander and serve in bowls.

Nutrition notes per serving: *272 Calories, Protein 19g, Carbohydrate 17g, Fat 15g, Saturated fat 5g, Fibre 2g, Added sugar 0g, Salt 0.93g.*

TIP

Tamarind, the pulp that fills the pod and surrounds the seeds of the tropical tamarind tree, is usually sold in a rectangular block complete with seeds, which are as hard as small black stones. You usually mix the pulp with warm water and pick out the seeds. The paste can then be used in many types of curries, where its acid and scented flavour acts like the juice of citrus fruits, lime or lemon, both of which can be used as an alternative. Tamarind is now also available ready-prepared in jars.

STIR-FRIED PRAWNS ⓕ

1 tsp Sichuan peppercorns

½ tsp black peppercorns

1 tbsp groundnut oil

3 spring onions, white and green parts separated, finely sliced

2.5cm/1in piece fresh root ginger, finely chopped

4 garlic cloves, finely chopped

450g/1lb peeled raw prawns

1 tsp dry sherry or rice wine (See Tip, page 37)

1 tbsp light soy sauce

2 tbsp chilli bean sauce (See Tip)

225g/8oz tomatoes, skinned and sliced

½ tsp sugar

1 Grind together the Sichuan and black peppercorns in a clean coffee grinder or with a pestle and mortar. Place the oil in a wok and stir fry the ground peppercorns with the white part of the spring onions, the ginger and the garlic for 1 minute.

2 Add the prawns and stir for 1 minute, then add the sherry or rice wine, soy sauce, chilli bean sauce, tomatoes and sugar. Cover and cook for 3 minutes. Sprinkle with the green part of the onions to serve.

Nutrition notes per serving: *144 Calories, Protein 21g, Carbohydrate 6g, Fat 4g, Saturated fat 1g, Fibre 1g, Added sugar 1g, Salt 1.09g.*

TIP

Chilli bean sauce can be bought at Chinese grocers or in many supermarkets but, if you can't get hold of it, mix together yellow bean sauce and chilli sauce. If you want to make the dish even hotter, add a few finely chopped red chillies.

WHELK FRITTERS

Serves 4

8–10 cooked whelks

2 medium eggs, separated

2 plum tomatoes, skinned, seeded and chopped

55g/2oz onion, very finely chopped

2 garlic cloves, very finely chopped

2 tbsp chopped fresh parsley

40g/1½oz Matzo meal or fresh breadcrumbs

salt and freshly ground black pepper

sunflower oil, for frying

lemon wedges, to serve

1 Remove the cooked whelks from their shells (you will need about 55g/2oz) and roughly chop. Place the egg yolks in a bowl and lightly break up with a fork. Stir in the whelks, tomatoes, onion, garlic, parsley, Matzo meal or breadcrumbs and salt and pepper to taste.

2 In another bowl, whisk the egg whites into soft peaks, then gently fold into the main fritter mixture.

3 Pour a good layer of oil into a large heavy-based frying pan and leave over a high heat until very hot. Lower the temperature a little, then drop four large tablespoons of the whelk mixture into the pan and fry for 1½ minutes on each side until golden. Lift out on to kitchen paper and keep hot while you cook the remainder. You should end up with 12 fritters. Serve with lemon wedges.

Nutrition notes per serving: *257 Calories, Protein 7g, Carbohydrate 11g, Fat 21g, Saturated fat 3g, Fibre 1g, Added sugar 0g, Salt 0.63g.*

WARM OYSTERS WITH BLACK BEANS, GINGER AND CORIANDER

The oysters are opened, leaving about half the liquor that surrounds the oyster meats in the shell, then grilled until just set. The liquor gives a delightful salty tang to the sauce, but do discard half of it or the sauce will be too salty.

Serves 4

20 Pacific oysters, scrubbed

2.5cm/1in piece fresh root ginger, very finely chopped

7.5cm/3in piece cucumber

1 tbsp chopped fresh coriander

1 tsp snipped fresh chives

1 tbsp salted black beans, rinsed and roughly chopped, or black bean sauce (See Tip)

1 garlic clove, very finely chopped

1 tbsp dark soy sauce

2 tbsp dry sherry or rice wine (See Tip)

4 tbsp cold-pressed sesame oil

1   Open the oysters: wrap one hand in a tea towel and hold the oyster in it, with the more bowl-shaped half of the shell underneath and the flatter shell on top. Take an oyster knife or small, thick-bladed knife in your other hand. Push the point of the knife into the hinge of the oyster, located at the narrowest point. Work the knife forwards and backwards between the two halves of the shell to break the hinge. As the hinge breaks, twist the point of the knife to lever the top shell upwards.

2   Now slide the knife under the top shell to sever the ligament that joins the oyster to the shell. The ligament is slightly right of centre in the shell. Lift off the top shell, trying not to let any fragments fall on to the oyster and keeping the bottom shell upright so as not to lose any of the juice. Pick out any little pieces of shell that might have broken off into the oyster.

3   Pour away half the oyster liquor surrounding the meat in each shell and nestle the oysters in the grill pan so that they can't roll over during cooking. Sprinkle each one with the chopped ginger and set aside.

4   Cut the cucumber into 2.5cm/1in pieces, then thinly slice each piece and cut lengthways into matchstick-width shreds. Mix with the coriander and chives.

5   Preheat the grill to hot. Place the salted black beans or black bean sauce in a small pan with the garlic, soy sauce, sherry or rice wine and sesame oil. Leave over a very low heat to warm through.

6   Grill the oysters for 3 minutes until they plump up and the meat is just set. Arrange on four warm plates and spoon over a little of the sauce, then sprinkle a little of the cucumber mixture over each one.

Nutrition notes per serving: *183 Calories, Protein 15g, Carbohydrate 2g, Fat 12g, Saturated fat 2g, Fibre 1g, Added sugar trace, Salt 2.21g.*

TIP

If you can get the fermented and salted black beans available in Chinese food shops you will be glad I suggested trying, because they keep for ages and are a great addition to so many stir-fry dishes. However, these oysters are also well worth preparing with black bean sauce; try and get the type with whole black beans in it rather than the smooth one. Rice wine, made from glutinous rice, yeast and water, is usually only available from Chinese supermarkets. A dry or fino sherry makes a good substitute.

Main Courses

FRITTO MISTO DI MARE

This is my version of the classic Italian dish where small pieces of seafood are tossed in seasoned flour, then deep-fried in olive oil. Much as I've enjoyed this dish on many occasions, I've always baulked at putting it in a recipe book because of the high price of olive oil – there's no point in writing recipes if you have a suspicion that nobody is ever going to cook them. However, I spent some time trying to work out the minimum amount of oil you'd need to deep-fry four portions of this superb dish successfully, and I now present my own version of *fritto misto*, specially adapted to use just one bottle of olive oil.

Serves 4

12 large raw prawns

8 prepared scallops (See Tip)

115g/4oz prepared squid (See Tip, page 42)

salt

1 litre/1¾ pints olive oil

85g/3oz plain flour, seasoned with salt and black pepper

2 lemon wedges, to serve

1 Preheat the oven to 150C/300F/Gas 2. Line a large baking tray with plenty of kitchen paper.

2 Shell the prawns: hold the head and tail end of each prawn and pull off the head. Place your thumbnails under the shell on the underside and peel off. Remove the tail shell or leave it on if you prefer. Using the point of a sharp knife, remove the black intestinal vein that runs down the back.

3 Detach the coral from each scallop and slice it in half lengthways (this prevents it from exploding during cooking). Slice the scallop meat horizontally in half as well. Cut the squid across into thick rings. Season all the seafood with a little salt.

4 Pour the oil into a large pan and heat to 190C/375F/Gas 5 or until a small piece of white bread dropped into the oil browns and rises to the surface within a minute. Toss the seafood in the seasoned flour and deep-fry in batches for 30 seconds–1 minute, until the floury coating is just beginning to be tinged with brown. Using a slotted spoon, lift out and place on the baking tray and keep hot in the oven while you cook the remainder. Serve with the lemon wedges.

Nutrition notes per serving: *368 Calories, Protein 32g, Carbohydrate 17g, Fat 19g, Saturated fat 3g, Fibre 1g, Added sugar 0g, Salt 1.11g.*

TIP

To prepare scallops: wash in plenty of cold water. Hold the scallop, flat shell uppermost, and slide a thick-bladed knife between the shells. Keeping the blade flat against the top shell, feel for the ligament that joins the shell to the muscle meat of the scallop and cut through it. Lift off the top shell, cut and pull out and discard the black stomach sac and the frilly 'skirt', which surrounds the white scallop meat and bright orange coral (roe). Wash well to remove sand and grit. Cut the scallop meat away from the bottom shell. Pull off and discard the small white ligament that is attached to the side of the scallop meat.

CRAB AND SPINACH CANNELLONI WITH BASIL AND TOMATO SAUCE

Rolls of pasta stuffed with flaked white crab meat and spinach, topped with a rich tomato sauce with plenty of basil, then sprinkled with grated Parmesan cheese and browned under the grill – what could be nicer? I can't claim that this is an authentic Italian recipe, it's one of mine, but all I've done is substitute crab for meat in a classic cannelloni and added some basil to the sauce. I think it is almost better than the traditional version. You can use fresh, pasteurised or thawed frozen crab meat.

Serves 4

115g/4oz fresh spinach, washed and large stalks removed

25g/1oz butter

225g/8oz white crab meat

50g/2oz brown crab meat

pinch of freshly grated nutmeg (See Tip)

pinch of cayenne pepper (See Tip)

salt and freshly ground black pepper

8 sheets fresh lasagne

20g/¾oz Parmesan cheese, finely grated

FOR THE TOMATO SAUCE

1 onion, finely chopped

1 garlic clove, finely chopped

2 tbsp olive oil

400g can chopped tomatoes

50ml/2fl oz red wine vinegar

2 tsp caster sugar

salt and freshly ground black pepper

10 fresh basil leaves, thinly shredded

1   Make the sauce: fry the onion and garlic in the olive oil for 5 minutes until softened. Add the tomatoes and simmer for 15–20 minutes. Meanwhile, place the vinegar and sugar in a separate pan and boil down until reduced to about one teaspoon. Stir into the tomato sauce and season with salt and pepper. Add the basil and set aside.

2   Preheat the oven to 190C/375F/Gas 5. Shake off any excess water on the spinach leaves and place in a pan and cook over a high heat for 2 minutes until wilted. Drain well, chop finely and return to the pan with the butter. Cook for 1 minute until all the excess moisture has evaporated, then stir in the crab meat and season with the nutmeg, cayenne and salt and pepper.

3   Bring 1.7 litres/3 pints of water and one tablespoon of salt to the boil in a large pan. Add the lasagne, take the pan off the heat, cover and leave for 5 minutes. Drain the pasta and lay out on plastic film.

4   Spoon some of the crab mixture along one short end of each lasagne sheet and roll up. Lay the rolls side by side, seam-side down, in a lightly greased shallow ovenproof dish. Spoon over the tomato sauce, sprinkle over the Parmesan and bake for 20 minutes or until golden.

Nutrition notes per serving: *357 Calories, Protein 22g, Carbohydrate 31g, Fat 17g, Saturated fat 6g, Fibre 3g, Added sugar 3g, Salt 1.36g.*

TIP

Try to use freshly grated whole nutmeg to obtain the best flavour. Ground nutmeg tends to lose its warm, sweet nutty flavour quite quickly. Don't be too heavy-handed when seasoning with cayenne pepper. It is prepared from the smallest hottest chillies, and packs a powerful punch.

STUFFED SQUID

This is the classic Greek recipe for stuffing the bodies of squid or cuttlefish. You will need to use medium-size squid with a body section measuring 13–15cm/5–6in in length.

Serves 4

8 squid (See Tip)

55g/2oz pine nuts

1 onion, finely chopped

2 garlic cloves, finely chopped

4 tbsp olive oil

85g/3oz long grain rice

25g/1oz raisins

2 tbsp chopped fresh flatleaf parsley

400g can chopped tomatoes

2 sun-dried tomatoes in oil, drained and finely chopped

125ml/4fl oz dry white wine

sea salt and freshly ground black pepper

1 Preheat the oven to 180C/350F/Gas 4. Clean the squid (See Tip), taking care not to split the pouches. Rub the outside of the pouches liberally with one teaspoon of salt, leave for 5 minutes, then rinse well with cold water. Chop the tentacles into small pieces.

2 Spread the pine nuts over a baking tray and toast in the oven for about 7 minutes or until lightly browned. Remove from the oven and set aside.

3 Fry the onion and garlic in half the olive oil for 5 minutes until softened and lightly browned. Add the chopped squid tentacles and fry for 3 minutes. Stir in the rice, pine nuts, raisins and parsley, and season with salt and pepper. Leave to cool slightly, then spoon into the squid pouches, making sure they are only two-thirds full to allow room for the rice to swell up. Secure each one with a cocktail stick.

4 Heat the remaining oil in a large flameproof casserole dish. Add the squid and fry for a few minutes on all sides until lightly browned. Add the tomatoes, sun-dried tomatoes, wine, salt and pepper, then cover and bake for 1 hour. Remove the cocktail sticks and serve hot or cold.

Nutrition notes per serving: *441 Calories, Protein 21g, Carbohydrate 30g, Fat 25g, Saturated fat 3g, Fibre 2g, Added sugar 0g, Salt 1.22g.*

TIP

To prepare squid: grasp the head in one hand and the body in another. Gently pull the head and it should come away easily, taking the milky white intestines with it. You may like to retain the ink sac which will be in the intestines – it is pearly-white with a slight blue tinge. On larger squid, you can also save the two pieces of muscle running down either side of the intestines. The rest of the intestines can be discarded. Cut off the tentacles from the head, discard the head. Squeeze out the beak-like mouth from the centre of the tentacles, cut it off and discard it. The tentacles can either be separated or left intact. Reach into the body and pull out the plastic-like quill and the soft white roe, if there is any. Pull off the two fins from either side of the body pouch, then pull away the purple, semi-transparent skin from both the body and the fins. Wash the pouch out with water.

CAUTION! This recipe contains nuts.

SPRING ROLLS WITH SQUID, CRAB, BEANSPROUTS AND SHIITAKE MUSHROOMS

The filling is briefly stir fried, then rolled up in spring-roll wrappers and deep-fried. This is not an authentic recipe but spring rolls are such a good idea and generally I find the fillings a bit dull – often little more than cabbage, beansprouts and soy sauce. I think seafood and oriental mushrooms work rather well, but you could also try shredded green summer cabbage, pork, shredded cooked skate with soy sauce, a pinch or two of star anise and some finely diced red chilli.

Makes 12

115g/4oz prepared squid (See Tip, page 42)

6 spring onions

2 tbsp toasted sesame oil

2 garlic cloves, finely chopped

1cm/½in piece fresh root ginger, finely chopped

175g/6oz pork escalope, cut into 10cm/4in-long strips

115g/4oz beansprouts

55g/2oz shiitake mushrooms, thinly sliced

175g/6oz white crab meat

1 tbsp dark soy sauce

pinch of caster sugar

1 tsp salt

freshly ground Sichuan pepper

2 tbsp plain flour

12 large spring-roll wrappers (See Tip)

sunflower oil, for deep-frying

FOR THE DIPPING SAUCE

2 tbsp dark soy sauce

1 tbsp sweet chilli sauce

2.5cm/1in piece fresh root ginger, finely grated

1 garlic clove, very finely chopped

1 small red finger chilli, seeded and very finely chopped

1 tbsp chopped fresh coriander

1 Slit the squid pouch open along one side and cut it into thin strips about 10cm/4in long. Cut the spring onions into 7.5cm/3in lengths, then cut lengthways into fine shreds.

2 Heat the sesame oil in a wok or large frying pan, add the garlic and ginger and stir fry for a few seconds. Add the squid and pork and stir fry over a high heat for 3 minutes. Add the beansprouts and mushrooms and stir fry for 30 seconds only. Tip into a bowl and gently stir in the spring onions, crab meat, soy sauce, sugar, salt and Sichuan pepper. In another bowl, mix the flour with two tablespoons of cold water to make a paste.

3 Fill the spring-roll wrappers: place a wrapper on a work surface with one corner facing you. Keep the other wrappers covered with a slightly damp cloth to prevent them drying out. Place three heaped teaspoons of filling in a line about 5cm/2in from the corner. Fold the corner over the line of filling and give it a little roll, making sure that the filling stays in place. Fold in one side of the wrapper, then the other side, so that they overlap in the centre and the filling is completely enclosed. Roll up tightly, holding in the sides as you do so. Seal the end with a little of the flour-and-water paste. Repeat for the remaining spring rolls, keeping them covered with a damp cloth.

4 Pour the oil into the pan, so that it is about one-third full and heat to 190C/375F/Gas 5 or until a small piece of white bread dropped into the oil browns and rises to the surface within a minute. Deep-fry the spring rolls, four at a time, for 5–6 minutes until crisp and golden. They tend to float in the oil, so a good trick is to rest a frying basket or metal sieve on top of them to keep them submerged during cooking.

5 Mix together the dipping-sauce ingredients with one tablespoon of water and pour into small bowls or saucers and serve with the hot spring rolls.

Nutrition notes per serving: *215 Calories, Protein 10g, Carbohydrate 19g, Fat 11g, Saturated fat 2g, Fibre trace, Added sugar 1g, Salt 1.74g.*

TIP

Spring-roll wrappers are available from Chinese supermarkets and some well-stocked delicatessens. You can use filo pastry if you prefer.

FILLET OF TURBOT WITH CLAMS,
COCKLES AND CHARDONNAY

The clams and cockles are steamed open in a rich Chardonnay, then a butter sauce is made with the cooking liquor and plenty of flatleaf parsley. I thought up this dish as an attractive way of using the small clams called butterfish that live at one end of the estuary and the small cockles that live at the other, combining them in a main course with that magnificent fish, the turbot. The steamed turbot fillets are served covered in the parsley and butter sauce with cockles and clams both in and out of the shells, the idea being to use some of the shells as a garnish.

Serves 4

4 x 175g/6oz pieces turbot fillet, skin on

salt

2 shallots, finely chopped

90ml/3fl oz Chardonnay wine, preferably Australian

16 small clams, such as carpetshell or cherrystone clams, scrubbed and washed

20 cockles, scrubbed and washed

300ml/½ pint Fish stock (page 62)

175g/6oz chilled unsalted butter, cut into small pieces

2 tbsp chopped fresh flatleaf parsley

1 If you don't have a steamer big enough for cooking the turbot, take a very large pan into which a dinner plate will fit, and put some sort of trivet in the bottom, such as a small upturned bowl. Add about 5cm/2in water and bring to the boil. Season the turbot fillets lightly with salt and place them on the plate. Rest this on the trivet, cover and steam the fish for 10 minutes.

2 Meanwhile, place the shallots, Chardonnay, clams and cockles into a pan. Cover and cook over a high heat, shaking the pan every now and then, for 2–3 minutes, until the clams have opened. Discard any that remain closed.

3 Strain the shellfish through a colander set over a shallow pan, keeping back the last tablespoon or so of liquid as this may contain some grit and should be discarded. Shell half the clams and cockles. Add the fish stock to the shellfish cooking liquor and boil rapidly until reduced to about six tablespoons. Whisk in the butter, a piece at a time. Return all the shellfish to the sauce with the parsley and heat through.

4 Place the turbot fillets on to four warm plates and pour over the sauce. Rearrange the shells so they look attractive.

Nutrition notes per serving: *547 Calories, Protein 39g, Carbohydrate 3g, Fat 41g, Saturated fat 24g, Fibre trace, Added sugar 0g, Salt 3.70g.*

TIP

If you can't get small live clams and cockles, use mussels instead. We quite often do the dish with mussels in the restaurant.

PRAWN JAMBALAYA

Jambalaya comes from New Orleans and is based on paella but the Spanish settlers, being unable to get saffron and olive oil, used local produce. Their combination of green peppers, celery and onions produced what is now known as the 'holy trinity', the flavour that most typifies Creole cookery. This is delicious served with a green salad.

Serves 6

50ml/2fl oz vegetable oil

115g/4oz *kabanos* (smoked Spanish sausage) sliced

2 tsp paprika

8 garlic cloves, chopped

1 onion, chopped

2 green peppers, seeded and chopped

4 celery sticks, sliced

2 red chillies, seeded and finely chopped

450g/1lb boneless skinless chicken breasts, cut into 2.5cm/1in pieces

450g/1lb raw peeled prawn tails (See Tip)

2 fresh bay leaves, thinly sliced, or 2 dried bay leaves, crushed

1 fresh thyme sprig, chopped

1 tsp chopped fresh oregano, or ½ tsp dried oregano

450g/1lb long grain rice

1.2 litres/2 pints chicken stock

1 tsp salt

3 spring onions, sliced

pinch of chilli powder (optional)

1 Heat the oil in a large frying pan or any other large shallow skillet-type dish and gently fry the *kabanos*. Add the paprika and stir to colour the oil.

2 Toss in the garlic and sweat a little, then add the onion, green peppers, celery and red chillies. Cook over a medium heat until the moisture has been driven off and the vegetables are beginning to colour.

3 Add the chicken, prawns, bay leaves, thyme and oregano and cook over a medium heat for 5 minutes. Add the rice and stir for 2 minutes, then pour in the chicken stock and add the salt. Bring to the boil, then reduce the heat and simmer gently for 15 minutes or until all the liquid has been absorbed by the rice. Stir in the spring onions and taste. If you like things hot, add some chilli powder.

Nutrition notes per serving: *571 Calories, Protein 42g, Carbohydrate 71g, Fat 15g, Saturated fat 3g, Fibre 2g, Added sugar 0g, Salt 2.86g.*

TIP

Raw prawn tails are now available in most supermarkets. For extra flavour in the Jambalaya, fry the shells in about 50ml/2fl oz of vegetable oil, then pass the oil through a sieve into the pan just before adding the rice.

CRAB, SAFFRON AND LEEK QUICHE

Serves 4

225g/8oz shortcrust pastry (recipe below)

115g/4oz leeks, thinly sliced

pinch of saffron strands, soaked in 1 tbsp warm water (See Tip)

15g/½oz unsalted butter

300ml/½ pint Fish stock (page 62)

30ml/1fl oz Noilly Prat or other dry vermouth

squeeze of fresh lemon juice

salt

pinch of cayenne pepper

3 eggs

125ml/4fl oz double cream

175g/6oz white crab meat

1 Preheat the oven to 190C/375F/Gas 5. Roll out the pastry and line a deep 20cm/8in flan ring or flan case. Prick the pastry, cover with greaseproof paper and fill with baking beans. Bake for 10 minutes, then remove the beans and paper and leave to cool.

2 Boil the leek slices in lightly salted water for 10 minutes until really soft. Drain and place in a pan. Add the soaked saffron with the butter and drive off the excess moisture by stirring over a high heat.

3 Boil the fish stock and Noilly Prat together over a high heat to reduce to about 2 tablespoons of liquid. Add the lemon juice, salt and cayenne pepper to taste, then beat into the eggs and cream.

4 Line the pastry case with the leeks and sprinkle the crab meat over the top. Pour over the eggs and cream mixture and bake for 20 minutes until golden. Serve hot or cold.

Nutrition notes per serving including pastry: *776 Calories, Protein 21g, Carbohydrate 46g, Fat 57g, Saturated fat 30g, Fibre 2g, Added sugar trace, Salt 2.07g.*

TIP

Saffron, the most expensive spice in the world, is the dried stigmas of the purple-flowering saffron crocus. To yield 450g/1lb of saffron takes up to a quarter of a million flowers, all harvested by hand. It is mainly imported from Spain and has an aromatic, slightly bitter taste. Only a few threads are needed to flavour and colour dishes. The threads are usually soaked in a little hot liquid before being added to a dish to extract the flavour and brilliant yellow colour. Powdered saffron is also available, though not quite as good.

SHORTCRUST PASTRY

Makes enough for 1 x 20cm/8in flan case

225g/8oz plain flour

½ tsp salt

70g/2½oz butter, cut into pieces

70g/2½oz lard, cut into pieces

1 Sift the flour and salt into a food processor, add the butter and lard and process until the mixture resembles fine breadcrumbs. (Alternatively, sift into a bowl and rub the fats into the flour with your fingers.)

2 Tip into a large mixing bowl and stir in 1½ tablespoons of cold water with a round-bladed knife until everything starts to stick together. Bring together into a ball, turn out on to a work surface lightly dusted with flour and knead once or twice until smooth. Cover and chill for 20 minutes or until you are ready to use it.

LOBSTER POT PIE

This is a fish pie from the other side of the Atlantic, where lobsters are cheap and plentiful. I wouldn't expect you to use one of our British lobsters, they're far too expensive, but you can use cheaper North American lobsters.

Serves 8

1 cooked lobster, weighing about 675g/1½lb

1 quantity Shellfish stock (See Tip), made with the broken lobster shell

350g/12oz small waxy potatoes, such as Charlotte, thickly sliced

115g/4oz whole baby carrots

115g/4oz fresh young peas

225g/8oz cod fillet, cut into 1cm/½in-thick slices

55g/2oz butter

1 onion, chopped

40g/1½oz plain flour

150ml/¼ pint double cream

salt and freshly ground black pepper

FOR THE PASTRY

350g/12oz plain flour

¾ tsp salt

115g/4oz butter, cut into small pieces

1 egg yolk, beaten with 1 tsp milk

1 Remove the meat from the cooked lobster (See Tip, page 18). Cut the lobster tail meat into 1cm/½in-thick slices. Break up the lobster shell and use to make the stock (See Tip).

2 Strain the stock into a clean pan, add the potatoes and carrots and simmer for 5 minutes or until just cooked. Add the peas and simmer for 1 minute. Remove the vegetables using a slotted spoon. Add the cod to the pan and simmer for 1 minute, then lift out and set aside. You need 600ml/1 pint of stock for the sauce. If you have more, boil rapidly until reduced.

3 Melt the butter in a pan, add the onion and cook for 5 minutes or until lightly browned. Stir in the flour and cook for 1 minute. Remove the pan from the heat and gradually stir in the stock. Return to the heat and bring to the boil, stirring all the time. Simmer for 5 minutes, then stir in the cream, lobster meat, cod and vegetables. Season and transfer to a 1.75-litre/3-pint pie dish. Push a pie funnel into the centre of the mixture, if using one. Set aside to cool.

4 Make the pastry: sift the flour and salt into a food processor, add the butter and process until the mixture resembles fine breadcrumbs. Transfer to a mixing bowl and stir in two tablespoons of cold water with a round-bladed knife until everything starts to stick together. Bring together in a ball, turn out on to a lightly floured work surface and knead once or twice until smooth.

5 Roll out the pastry thinly until it is about 2.5cm/1in bigger than the top of the pie dish. Cut a thin strip from around the edge, brush with a little water and press on to the rim of the pie dish. Brush the top of the pastry strip with a little more water. Make a small cut in the centre of the remaining pastry, then lay it over the pie so that the funnel pokes through the cut. Press it on to the rim of the dish and crimp the edge with your fingers. Brush the egg and milk mixture over the pie top, then bake for 35–40 minutes until the pastry is golden. If it starts to over-brown, protect the edge of the pastry with a strip of foil.

Nutrition notes per serving: *544 Calories, Protein 20g, Carbohydrate 50g, Fat 31g, Saturated fat 18g, Fibre 3g, Added sugar 0g, Salt 1.87g.*

TIP

For the shellfish stock: fry 55g/2oz each of chopped carrot, onion and celery in 15g/½oz unsalted butter for 2–3 minutes. Add the broken lobster shell and one tablespoon of cognac and fry for 2 minutes. Add two tablespoons of white wine, one teaspoon of chopped fresh tarragon, 85g/3oz roughly chopped tomato, 1.2 litres/2 pints of Fish stock (page 62) and a pinch of cayenne pepper and simmer for 40 minutes. Strain through a sieve lined with muslin.

Salads

SEARED SCALLOP SALAD WITH PARMA HAM AND CROÛTONS

A simple salad of young leaves with scallops, strips of Parma ham and granary-bread croûtons, finished with a few snipped chives. The scallops are sautéed in a hot frying pan in which a very small amount of butter has been melted, giving them a really sweet, caramelised exterior. But they are only cooked briefly so that they remain succulent.

Serves 4

12 prepared scallops or 24 prepared queen scallops (See Tip, page 38)

salt and freshly ground black pepper

35g/1¼oz unsalted butter

3 x 1cm/½in-thick slices granary bread, crusts removed and cut into 1cm/½in dice

100g bag mixed baby-leaf salad

8 slices Parma ham, cut into 2cm/¾in side strips

1 quantity Mustard dressing (See Tip)

1 tsp walnut oil

½ tbsp snipped fresh chives

1 If using the larger scallops, slice horizontally into two discs. Leave queen scallops whole. Season with a little salt and pepper and set aside.

2 Make the croûtons: melt 25g/1oz of the butter in a frying pan, add the bread cubes and fry for a few minutes, turning them over as they brown. Using a slotted spoon, lift out and drain on kitchen paper.

3 Arrange the salad leaves on four plates. Heat a frying pan until very hot and melt the remaining butter, then add the scallops and fry for just 30 seconds on each side. Remove from the pan and tuck them in among the salad leaves.

4 Add the strips of Parma ham and the croûtons to the pan and fry briskly over a high heat for just a few seconds to warm through. Sprinkle over the salad. Add the Mustard dressing and walnut oil to the pan, bring to the boil, stir in the chives and taste for seasoning, then drizzle over the salad.

Nutrition notes per serving: *525 Calories, Protein 42g, Carbohydrate 12g, Fat 34g, Saturated fat 9g, Fibre 1g, Added sugar 0g, Salt 3.72g.*

TIP

To make Mustard dressing: whisk together 90ml/3fl oz sunflower oil, one tablespoon white wine vinegar, half a teaspoon of salt, half a finely chopped shallot, half a finely chopped garlic clove and one teaspoon of made English mustard. You can also make the dressing by placing all the ingredients in a screw-top jar and shaking well to combine. This dressing goes very well with bitter leaves such as chicory, dandelions and radicchio. It can be made some time in advance. The snipped fresh chives add an extra dimension to the flavour.

CAUTION! This recipe contains nuts (oil).

FRESH CRAB SALAD WITH TARRAGON MAYONNAISE, CUCUMBER AND ENDIVE

This is based on a similar salad I ate in a restaurant in Dartmouth and is typical of the innovative cooking of the owner, Joyce Molyneux. It is best made with crab freshly picked from the shells, but if you don't want to be bothered simply buy fresh crab meat from your local fishmongers or fish counter at the supermarket.

Serves 4

225g/8oz white crab meat

115g/4oz brown crab meat

FOR THE TARRAGON MAYONNAISE

1 tsp each of finely chopped fresh parsley and tarragon

½ tsp ground star anise

½ quantity Olive oil mayonnaise (See page 13)

FOR THE CUCUMBER SALAD

½ cucumber

1 tsp chopped fresh parsley

1 tsp Thai fish sauce (*nam pla;* See Tip page 21)

juice and grated rind of 1 lime

FOR THE ENDIVE SALAD

50ml/2fl oz groundnut oil

1 tbsp white wine vinegar

½ tsp made English mustard

½ small garlic clove, finely chopped

½ shallot, finely chopped

1 tsp Quatre Epices (See Tip)

¼ tsp salt

2 handfuls endive leaves

1 Make the Tarragon mayonnaise: add the parsley, tarragon and star anise to the Olive oil mayonnaise.

2 Make the cucumber salad: peel the cucumber, cut it into segments lengthways, remove the seeds using a teaspoon and thinly slice. In a small bowl, mix together the parsley, fish sauce, lime juice and grated rind and 50ml/2fl oz of water. Pour over the cucumber and mix well.

3 Make the endive salad: place the oil, vinegar, mustard, garlic, shallot, Quatre Epices and salt in a bowl. Whisk together and use to dress the endive leaves.

4 Place a pile of crab meat on each plate with a dollop of mayonnaise, and a portion each of the cucumber and endive salads.

Nutrition notes per serving: *560 Calories, Protein 19g, Carbohydrate 2g, Fat 53g, Saturated fat 8g, Fibre 1g, Added sugar 0g, Salt 1.87g.*

TIP

To make Quatre Epices: mix together three-quarters of a teaspoon of freshly ground black pepper, one teaspoon of freshly grated nutmeg, three-quarters of a teaspoon of ground ginger and half a teaspoon of allspice. Store in a screw-top jar out of direct sunlight.

CAUTION! This recipe contains nuts (oil).

RICE-SHAPED PASTA WITH SEAFOOD, ROCKET AND ROASTED VEGETABLES

I have seen rice-shaped pasta sold as *puntalette*, *puntine* and *orzo*. Made to look like rice, it provides a bit of a culinary joke, if you like, because a lot of people will think they're eating a rice salad and then be surprised to find they're not.

TV Cooks **RICK STEIN COOKS SEAFOOD**

Serves 4

350g/12oz rice-shaped pasta

1 small aubergine, cut into 2.5cm/1in cubes

1 red onion, cut into thin wedges

1 red pepper, seeded and cut into 2.5cm/1in pieces

1 plum tomato, cut into thin wedges

2 garlic cloves, finely chopped

90ml/3fl oz extra virgin olive oil

½ tsp coarse sea salt

3–4 tbsp white wine or water

450g/1lb mussels, cleaned (See Tip, page 17)

115g/4oz prepared squid, cut into rings (See Tip, page 42)

salt and freshly ground black pepper

115g/4oz cooked peeled North Atlantic prawns, thawed if frozen

3 sun-dried tomatoes in oil, thinly sliced

1 red finger chilli, seeded and finely chopped

25g/1oz Parmesan cheese, finely grated

1 tbsp white wine vinegar

5 tbsp chopped fresh parsley

55g/2oz rocket (See Tip)

1 Preheat the oven to 220C/425F/Gas 7. Bring 1.75 litres/3 pints of water and one tablespoon of salt to the boil in a large pan. Add the pasta and cook for 9 minutes or until *al dente*, then drain and leave to cool.

2 Meanwhile, place the aubergine, onion, red pepper and tomato in a bowl with the garlic, two tablespoons of the olive oil and the sea salt and mix together well. Spread out in a small roasting tin and roast for 30 minutes, or until well coloured around the edges. Remove from the heat and leave to cool.

3 Place the wine or water in a pan, add the mussels, then cover and cook over a high heat for 3–4 minutes until they open. Discard any that remain closed. Shell the mussels and leave to cool.

4 Heat one tablespoon of the olive oil in a frying pan. Add the squid and fry over a high heat for 2½ minutes until lightly browned. Season with salt and pepper and leave to cool.

5 When the pasta, roasted vegetables, mussels and squid are all cold, place them in a large bowl with the remaining olive oil, the prawns, sun-dried tomatoes, chilli, Parmesan, vinegar, four tablespoons of parsley, one teaspoon of salt and 10 turns of the black pepper mill. Toss together lightly, then fold in the rocket. Spoon the salad on to a large serving platter and sprinkle with the remaining parsley.

Nutrition notes per serving: *683 Calories, Protein 31g, Carbohydrate 73g, Fat 31g, Saturated fat 5g, Fibre 6g, Added sugar 6g, Salt 2.86g.*

TIP

Rocket, an old-fashioned salad herb, has long been popular in Mediterranean countries. It has long spear-like leaves that resemble radish or young turnip tops, and a slightly bitter peppery taste.

SAUTÉED SQUID WITH GREEK SALAD

The squid is cooked very simply with a little thyme, garlic and dried chilli, then served with one of my favourite salads – Greek salad, made with feta cheese, cucumber, tomatoes, olives and onion in a good olive oil dressing. Greek salad is usually fairly rustic, with the ingredients in rough chunks, but here they are cut very small so that the salad looks neat on the plate with the squid.

Serves 4

350g/12oz prepared small squid (See Tip, page 42)

2 tbsp olive oil

2 fresh thyme sprigs

1 garlic clove, finely chopped

pinch of dried chilli flakes

good pinch of sea salt

10 turns of the black pepper mill

FOR THE GREEK SALAD

2 salad tomatoes, skinned, seeded and cut into 1cm/½in pieces

85g/3oz cucumber, cut into 1cm/½in pieces

55g/2oz feta cheese, cut into 1cm/½in pieces (See Tip)

1 small red onion, finely chopped

8 black olives with their stones

½ tbsp chopped fresh fennel herb or dill

FOR THE DRESSING

2 tbsp extra virgin olive oil

½ tbsp red wine vinegar

1 tsp retsina (optional)

1 Make the salad: place all the ingredients in a bowl and mix together gently. In another bowl, whisk together all the ingredients for the dressing and season to taste. Stir into the salad and set aside.

2 Cut the body of the squid into rings, the fins into strips and the tentacles into three. Heat the olive oil and thyme in a frying pan. When hot, add the squid and fry for 2½ minutes until just cooked. Add the garlic, chilli flakes, salt and pepper and toss for 1 minute, then serve immediately with the salad.

Nutrition notes per serving: *227 Calories, Protein 17g, Carbohydrate 5g, Fat 16g, Saturated fat 3g, Fibre 1g, Added sugar 0g, Salt 1.87g.*

TIP

Feta is a Greek cheese traditonally made from ewe's milk, but now more usually made from cow's milk. It is brilliant white with a firm, crumbly texture and a bland salty taste when young. It is stored in barrels of brine and the longer it is left the harder it becomes and it also develops a sourer, saltier flavour. It is normally found in vacuum packs in the chill cabinets of most supermarkets.

Basics

CORIANDER AND HAZELNUT BUTTER

Serves 4

85g/3oz hazelnuts

225g/8oz unsalted butter, softened

25g/1oz fresh coriander

15g/½ oz fresh parsley

25g/1oz shallot

juice of ½ lemon

freshly ground black pepper

1 Preheat the grill. Place the hazelnuts in the grill pan and roast, turning to ensure an even colouring. When the skins are dark brown, tip them on to one half of a tea towel, fold over the other half and roll off the skins. Open out the tea towel and roll the nuts to one side leaving the skins behind.

2 Place the hazelnuts in a food processor with the remaining ingredients and blend together. Transfer on to a piece of plastic film, roll into a sausage and chill until firm. This is an excellent stuffing for mussels.

CAUTION! This recipe contains nuts.

HOLLANDAISE SAUCE

Serves 4

225g/8oz unsalted butter

2 egg yolks

juice of ½ lemon, or to taste

good pinch of cayenne pepper

½ tsp salt

1 Clarify the butter by heating gently in a pan over a low heat, then skimming off any froth from the surface. Pour off the clear butter into a jug or pan, leaving behind the white solids on the bottom of the pan. Keep the clarified butter warm.

2 Place two tablespoons of water and the egg yolks in a heatproof bowl set over a pan of simmering water: make sure the base is not touching the water. Whisk the mixture until it has increased in volume and is creamy. Remove the pan from the heat and gradually whisk in the warm clarified butter a little at a time, building up an emulsion as if making mayonnaise. Add the lemon juice, the cayenne pepper and the salt. Use immediately. (If the sauce splits, take a clean pan, warm it and add one tablespoon of hot water, then slowly whisk in the curdled sauce.)

3 For a quick sauce: place the egg yolks, lemon juice and water in a liquidiser. Turn on and pour in the hot clarified butter, then season with cayenne pepper and salt.

CAUTION! This recipe contains partially cooked eggs.

FISH STOCK

Makes 1.2 litres/2 pints

1kg/2¼lb non-oily fish bones, including heads such as cod, sole, brill or plaice

25g/1oz button mushrooms, sliced

115g/4oz onion, chopped

115g/4oz carrot, chopped

115g/4oz celery, including the leafy top, chopped

1 tsp chopped fresh thyme

1 Place the fish bones in 2.25 litres/ 4 pints of water and bring to the boil. Simmer for 20 minutes, then strain through a sieve lined with muslin.

2 Return the stock to the pan and add the vegetables and thyme. Bring to the boil and simmer again for 40–45 minutes until reduced to about 1.2 litres/2 pints. Strain again. Season after the stock has been reduced. Store in a covered container in the fridge for up to four days. You can keep it indefinitely if you re-boil it every four days. Or store it in small quantities in the freezer.

Many of your favourite TV Cooks are also featured in a range of specially filmed half-hour BBC videos. They share the secrets of their key techniques and demonstrate some of their favourite recipes. Each video contains detailed step-by-step instructions on how to prepare and present creative dishes, acting as a companion to the book series.

The following are available as books and videos or as combined packs:

Ken Hom Cooks Chinese	BBCV5994
Mary Berry Cooks Cakes	BBCV6381
Mary Berry Cooks Puddings & Desserts	BBCV6193
Michael Barry Cooks Crafty Classics	BBCV6115
Nick Nairn Cooks The Main Course	BBCV6380
Rick Stein Cooks Fish	BBCV6111
Sophie Grigson Cooks Vegetables	BBCV6112
Valentina Harris Cooks Italian	BBCV6117

The following are only available as books:

Keith Floyd Cooks Barbies	0 563 38346 1
Ken Hom Cooks Noodles and Rice	0 563 38454 9
Madhur Jaffrey Cooks Curries	0 563 38794 7

INDEX